T0197468

Play-Bath-Bed

A Perfect Day for Baby

Pamela DiCarlantonio

Photos provided by Erin Morris Photography

AuthorHouse™
1663 Liberty Drive
Bloomington, IN 47403
www.authorhouse.com
Phone: 1 (833) 262-8899

This book is printed on acid-free paper.

ISBN: 978-1-7283-7206-8 (sc)
978-1-7283-7210-5 (hc)
978-1-7283-7205-1 (e)

Library of Congress Control Number: 2020916509

Print information available on the last page.

Published by AuthorHouse 10/08/2020

authorHOUSE®

For Meghan, Matt and Sweet Baby Lucas, in memory of Lucas'
Grandpa Mark who watches over him lovingly from Heaven

With heartfelt thanks to my sidekick and sounding board
on this special gift for Lucas (his amazing Aunt Andrea)

As you read aloud, the words in **italics** can be replaced with references to special people in <u>your</u> baby's life.

You can also personalize this book further by inserting your child's name in place of the word Baby and, if you choose, adding your own family photos at the end of each section.

Play

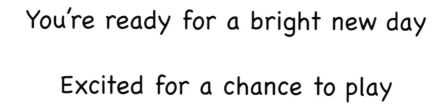

You're ready for a bright new day

Excited for a chance to play

With morning hugs and eating done

The time has come to have some fun

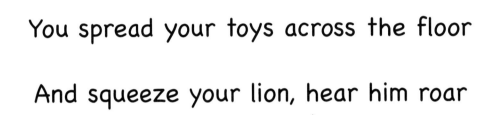

You spread your toys across the floor

And squeeze your lion, hear him roar

You build a castle with your blocks

Then add a moat with shiny rocks

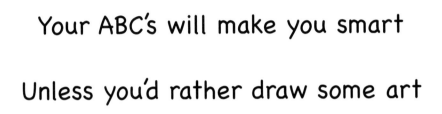

Your ABC's will make you smart

Unless you'd rather draw some art

You dance and sing your favorite song

With squeals of laughter all day long . . .

When too much playtime makes you cranky

Snuggle with your special blankie

Now it's time to get some rest

While feeling loved and very blessed!

My Playtime

It's a beautiful day, Baby
Just like you!

Bath

It's bathtime, Baby, time to scrub

And splash the bubbles in the tub

A time of day when you feel lucky

Playing with your Rubber Ducky

Safety is the biggest rule

The tub is like a mini pool

But **Mommy** never turns around

She's there to keep you safe and sound . . .

The water's warm and so are you

When bath is done, you're good as new

Snugly wrapped and squeaky clean

The cutest kid we've ever seen!

My Bathtime

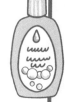

Clean or not,
you are always a blessing,
Baby!

Bed

It's nighttime, Baby, time for bed

Bath is over, books are read

Your bottle and your burp are done

The curtains block the setting sun

You hug your blanket and Teddy Bear tight

While **Daddy** blows kisses and

turns off the light . . .

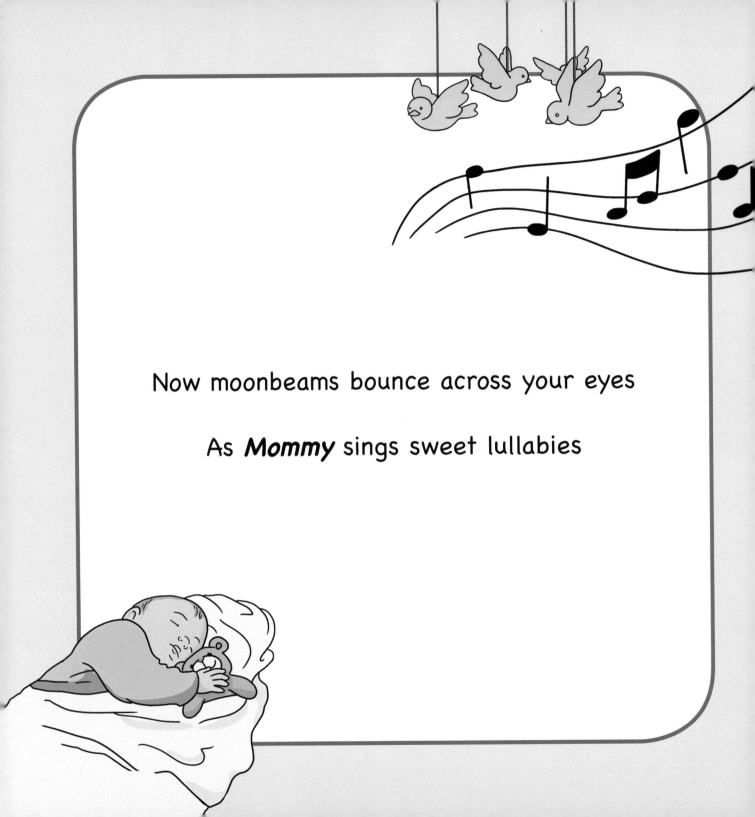

Now moonbeams bounce across your eyes

As **Mommy** sings sweet lullabies

You give your Bear a final squeeze

And settle in for bedtime Z's!

My Bedtime

Good night, Baby
Sleep tight!

Printed in the United States
By Bookmasters